Tennessee…the Volunteer State

We should celebrate our return to our corporate home….to a
state and a county full of richness and talent. As the
holidays approach and we move through our second year
back home, let this **Tennessean** serve as a reminder of this
great state and the partnerships we have created - corporation
to community and person to person.

We wish you and your families the most wonderful
Holiday Season 2000.

Sandy Beall
Sandy Beall

Robert McClenagan
Robert McClenagan

Ruby Tuesday

THIS BOOK IS MADE POSSIBLE
THROUGH THE GENEROUS SUPPORT OF OUR SPONSORS:

GAYLORD ENTERTAINMENT

Life Care Centers of America

COMDATA

A Ceridian Company

BRIDGESTONE Firestone

First American

EASTMAN

COLUMBIA

THE TENNESSEANS

A People Revisited

Photography by Robin Hood
Text by Barry Parker

THE TENNESSEANS: A People Revisited

For information, address: Parker Hood Press, Inc., 340 Crest Terrace
Drive, Chattanooga, TN 37404; phone: 423/622-8024

Library of Congress Catalog Card Number: 97-91850
ISBN: 0-9645704-2-4

Designed by Robertson Design, Inc., Brentwood, Tennessee
Printed in Hong Kong by Dai Nippon Printing Co., Ltd.
Published by Parker Hood Press, Inc., Chattanooga, Tennessee

FIRST EDITION

Previous spread: Blackberry Farm, Walland
This spread: Dog Tail Road, Moore County
Following spread: Moffitt Daylily Farm, Van Buren County

As he asked us all
to "find the good and praise it,"
we offer this book,
dedicated to the memory of
our beloved friend
and fellow Tennessean,
Alex Haley.

CONTENTS

Previous spread: Bonnie Carden, Anderson County

INTRODUCTION

Consider the iris. It blooms across Tennessee each spring, found alongside roads and fences and carefully tended in garden beds. It is common enough to be chosen the state flower, but that doesn't make an encounter with it any the less extraordinary. Take a moment to look. What do you see? An exotic flame of a plant that burns up and down in tongues of velvet color.

Seeing the extraordinary in the ordinary is what this book is about. Tennessee ravishes us with its common sights. Mountains, meadows, valleys, streams (running clear or silted coffee-color) and blowing green swaths of cropland: all are magic. So are people you chance to meet: at counter stools in cafes, at workbenches in shops, on their knees in the field, placing a hand to the soil as if to take its pulse. Often they speak with poetic feeling.

We ask you, dear reader, to shed your detachment as you turn these pages. Our wish is to have you enter Tennessee and have Tennessee enter you. We bid you share with the orchard owner the pride in his harvest, and look long into the eyes of the artist and musician and sculptor. We invite you to hear the auctioneer's chant as horses are trotted before the bidding crowd and feel the cool wash of thinning air as you stand on a fragrant peak among the spruce and fir.

Nearly two decades have passed since we set out the first time as photographer and writer to find Tennessee. During a journey that took six months and covered 25,000 miles, we searched for the images that convey this rich and varied place. With camera and pen, we collected our impressions. The result was THE TENNESSEANS: *A People And Their Land.* Governor Lamar Alexander, an eighth-generation Tennessean, proposed and personally financed our trip, wrote an introduction that dared to celebrate our differences as a people, and gave the project his loving attention.

Now, we have come again to Tennessee, to revisit the place we call home. Some of it, we find, has changed. There is less countryside, for one thing: pastures at the edges of towns have grown into subdivisions; sleepy stretches of road are now busy strips. In response, preservationists fight for historic buildings and forested knobs, lest they be lost in our growth and success. This struggle for balance makes us cherish our beauty, individuality and history all the more.

Many of the changes, though, delight us. Big cities have rediscovered their riverfronts; town squares have been rejuvenated; country stores have been reopened by a new generation of merchant. There are more festivals to enjoy, more parks, plazas and greenways to stroll, more highways to travel. There is more fine art in our museums, more blues on Beale Street, more seats in Neyland Stadium.

What we find constant is the friendliness, humor and good grace of Tennesseans, along with their deeply held values, their appreciation for the striving of others, and their attachment to the land. Though we came as strangers, they greeted us as cousins. Taking us in tow, they showed us about their workplaces and drove us across their countryside. Casting their gaze about them with a loving, proprietary air, they invited us into their lives.

This book represents a fresh gathering of impressions. We traveled separately this time, making individual discoveries, and there was no effort to have photographs and words coincide. Consequently, the pictures should be looked at for themselves and the words read for themselves. Yet, if you put all the images together, like bits of colored tile, and step back for a moment, a mosaic of the state will emerge.

Finally, this book makes no effort to be comprehensive or predictable. It is selective, subjective and lyrical. We have chosen the images that captivated us, delighted and surprised us, and always moved us, as we hope they do you. If you come to this work in order to sense and savor what this robust, sometimes fanciful, often contradictory place called Tennessee is about, this book will serve you, and you will find, as we did, that what we regard in Tennessee as ordinary is often extraordinary, indeed.

Robin Hood

Barry Parker

"IN THE RUSH OF WILDNESS, WE GROW CALM.
THE DELICATE MAKES US WHOLE."

Iris, Washington County

Right: Little Pigeon River, Great Smoky Mountains

THE MOUNTAINS TO THE RIVER

Let us go to Tennessee. We come, you and I, for the music and the mountains, the rivers and the cotton fields, the corporate towers and the country stores. We come for the greenest greens and the haziest blues and the muddiest browns on earth. We come for the hunters and storytellers, for the builders and worshipers. We come for dusty roads and turreted cities, for the smells of sweet potato pie and sweat of horses and men. We come for our quirkiness and our cleverness. We come to celebrate our common bonds and our family differences.

Let us begin in the forest-green wall of mountains we share with our neighbor to the east. We climb Roan Mountain's massive flank in a deepening mist. We spy the white state line that crosses the road at the place called Carver's Gap. We brace against the morning fog that spills across the gap. We sit for a while in the padded high grass. We visit the stand of blue spruce at the summit. Their needles are hung in silver pendants, a gift of the morning mist.

If we could but go high enough from here, we would slip beyond the fog into pure blue sky. From there we could see for hundreds of miles. Before us would be the staircase we descend before reaching the water that curls like smoke to form our border in the west. We would step from the high mountains onto plateaus so level and broad you forget there are valleys below. Next would come rolling green hills that rise and fall like ocean swells. Finally, we would stride the rich sultry flatland, ocean bottom once upon a time, and arrive at the serpentine river.

Descend from Roan into Sugar Hollow. Yawn and the sounds of the woods return. Travel through communities of rural homes that back up to wooded hillsides and newly plowed fields. At a distance, mountain ranges hang across the sky in powder blue curtains. A flatlander might feel hemmed by the broken horizon, deprived of the breath of long views. For natives, this tumbling land of peaks and hollows nourishes the soul.

This is fertile land for heroes. We come for the legendary frontiersman and the celebrated sergeant and the Nobel peacemaker. We come for presidents and statesmen and generals, some of them suckled in bare-walled cabins near mountain creeks.

We visit the tiny tailor shop with "A. Johnson" above the door. Here, a young unschooled tailor sat cross-legged on his bench, avidly debating politics with his Greene County neighbors. His wife taught him to write, and he rose from alderman and mayor to governor and congressman to Lincoln's vice president and successor in our country's most troubled time. Who better than the tailor to try and mend the rent garment of a nation?

We go north to glimpse the further past. It comes to us as a home on a grassy knob not far from Virginia. They call it Rocky Mount. It served as Tennessee's territorial capital before statehood arrived. A woman in homespun dress and apron greets us. She proffers a brick of tea for us to smell. "Look what Mr. Cobb brought back from Jonesboro," says his wife, Barsheba, proudly. We are in 1792 with the land's early settlers. They routed the British at Kings Mountain. They built forts and cabins, grist mills and inns. They added color to their world with marigold dyes and flavor with bricks of Chinese tea.

Their slightly gentrified speech and air reminds us we are near a border. What state has so many neighbors, each adding to the confluence of manners and ideas? Appalachian customs and crafts filter from the north and east, from Kentucky and North Carolina; the colonial order from Virginia. The Deep South percolates up from Mississippi, Alabama and Georgia. A whiff of the West comes to us from Arkansas and Missouri. And we enrich them in kind.

Our landscape divided us in The War, and still does. Cotton and slavery thrived in the open country of the middle and west. But many easterners, who lacked the large spreads and investment in slave labor, held with the North. How could we possibly march side by side? We were both staunch secessionists and fiery abolitionists; the last to leave the Union, the first to return.

1

We move west, leaving the peaks for canyons and plateaus. We observe the hands of our neighbors at work and play. We come for the old men fingering their cards at noon at Rose's grocery and the quick-fingered women planting flowers on embroidered spreads. We come for the hands that dart into the orchard trees, limbs heavy with ripened fruit. We come for the soot-laced hands of the last of the deep miners and for the farmer feeding grain into the noisy auger. We come for the hunter in the stand, testing the tension of the trigger. We come for the waving hand at the Jew's harp and the strumming hand at the guitar. We come for the fiddle maker, his hands quiet for a moment, fingers interlaced, while he sings of his craft.

Everywhere we travel is music. We dial it from the air. Gospel's joyful harmony brings visions of the Kingdom we will enter by and by. Its hand-clapping message transcends this world. Country sings of life's bittersweetness, of humor and heartache, in plain words and clever lyrics. The blues are not so much to be studied as felt. Forget the words; it's the emotion we're after. And all these musics spring from our soil and our experience. Now they belong to the world.

We leave the plateaus but keep our elevation. We want to see the middle land from above. We have traded drama for grace. The land rolls in domes of blue grass. You expect fine horses in such a land, and they are here, feeding in white-fenced pastures, pawing the ground in spacious stalls. You expect antebellum homes and Confederate monuments on the town square. You expect tradition and also enterprise in so fertile a land. Below us are the city of ambition's honeycombed spires.

We move further west into the countryside where we glimpse the Trace that carried frontier goods from Natchez on the Mississippi to Tennessee. We spot the monument to Meriwether Lewis, who died under mysterious circumstances at a tavern on the Trace. A state worker on a riding mower circles the explorer's grave as if to keep the spirit company.

We see Amish farms. A child of the sect sits at the edge of a field, watching his father plow behind two horses. The boy dangles bare feet from the high seat of a hayrake, like a sprite on a lily pad. He keeps his arm tucked to his side as he looks up and shyly returns our wave, bestowing on us the blessing of innocence.

We cross the river that carries our name and head into our final land. We seek its heart and find it in the first cool breath of fall. Below us stretches country as white as Colorado snowfields, and the smell of cotton is in the air. The roar of the gin comes to us. The seed bounces like corn in a popper and the lint flows in airy strands. A woman stands in a cotton field below us with her arms spread wide, her gesture proclaiming there is no finer sight and no finer place in the world.

We go northwest and join the migration. Herons and mallards and geese are moving south before a cold front. They find the strange bald-cypress lake, whose shallow water is so dense with plant life that its surface glows green as jade stone. With the birds, we follow the flyway along the western edge of the state. Below us, towboats grind against the river banked by levees as primal in form as prehistoric mounds.

We come to the city on the bluffs that still wears an Old South patina and set down on the wharf of stones polished by wagon wheels and toiling feet. Bales of cotton once were stacked here. The river runs brown and wide and hard before us. We stand in the golden dust of late afternoon light. It is a time when green fields glow across Tennessee and mountains loom in partly shadowed silence and any side road you pick leads to splendor. It is a time when we understand this land is too fine for you and me. That we don't own it. Rather, it possesses us.

Andrew Jackson statue, State Capitol

Left: State Capitol, Nashville

Pages 4 & 5: Grassy Bald, Roan Mountain
Pages 6 & 7: Smokehouse, Norris
Previous spread: John Rice Irwin garden, Norris

Moore County Courthouse, Lynchburg

Right: Philpot's Barber Shop, Winchester

Previous spread: Parthenon, Centennial Park, Nashville

University of Tennessee crew team, Tennessee River, Knoxville

Left: Europa and the Bull, University of Tennessee, Knoxville

John Sevier home, Knoxville

Hunter Art Museum, Chattanooga

Cotton covered in early snow, Rutherford County

Right: Mulberry Gap, Hancock County

Previous spread: Quarter horse wranglers, Leipers Fork, Williamson County

GINNINGS

	19 96	19 95
ALA	755,850	460,650
ARIZ	740,350	761,000
ARK	1,593,150	1,452,900
CALIF	2,327,300	2,247,300
FLA		
GA	2,041,500	1,908,900
KY		
LA	1,299,450	1,378,550
MISS	1,819,250	1,806,850
MO	557,250	477,400
N. MEX	75,150	55,800
N.C.	985,100	787,950
OKLA	126,100	117,250
S.C.	434,000	351,900
TENN	664,100	713,150
TEXAS	4,222,500	4,350,550
VA	153,000	128,200
OTHERS		
U.S.	510,150	354,650
TOTAL	18,435,550	17,468,500

COTTON LOAN PROGRAM

S ENDING	4-1-97
RIES	668
MPTIONS	94,076
ON ENTRIES	3,372,122
ON REDEMPTION	1,634,084
LOAN	1,738,038

ON HIGH	
ON LOW	
E MON	
TUES	
WED	
THURS	
FRI	
HIGH	
LOW	
CLOSE	

NONRAIN BROWN STOCK
DATE 4-14-97

MEMPHIS	1,836
GREENVILLE	0
GALVESTON	7,040
HOUSTON	95
NEW ORLEANS	0
TOTAL	8,971

CERT. STOCK
WEEKLY REPORT
DATE 4-14-97

MEMPHIS	116,267
GREENVILLE	0
GALVESTON	87,330
HOUSTON	18,323
NEW ORLEANS	0
DELIVERABLE 2	221,920

DAILY CERT. STOCK REPORT
ALL DELIVERY POINTS
DATE 4-14-97

ISSUED	3
CANCELLED	
DELIVERABLE # 2	221,920
AWAITING REVIEW	
DECERT. ORDERS	0
TO BE PROCESSED	

MEMPHIS
COTTON MOVEMENT
CONSUMPTION
1997 1996 19
1997 19 19
STATES
ACRES
UPLAND
FINAL
ALA
ARIZ
ARK
CALIF
FLA
GA
KY Kansas
LA
MISS
MO
N. M
N. C.
S. C.
OKLA
TENN
TEXAS
VA
OTHERS
TOTAL U.S.
ARIZONA
CALIFORNIA
NEW MEXICO
TEXAS
TOTAL PIMA
Feb. 97
CONSUMED 823,084
LINTERS
CONSUMED ALL KINDS 9,764,858
STOCKS CONSG. ESTB. 667,691
STOCK WAREHOUSE 9,097,167
SPINDLES ACTIVE 5,418
DOW JONES AVERAGE
VOLUME
CLOSE
STOCK
EXPORTS
DATE WK. END
1997
146,700
SHIPPED 251,800
6,149,200
3,998,400
3
4
5

"Not all that long ago, cotton was unloaded
at the cobble-stone wharf, carried by men and wagons
up the bluffs, and laid out farm-by-farm
on the tables of the Memphis brokers."

Mississippi River, near Memphis

Left: William Ousley, 50-year employee of Planters Gin, Memphis

Previous spread: Cotton Exchange, Memphis
Following spread: Highway 31, Williamson County

THE PLACE WE CALL HOME

We're puzzling over a grandfather's life. On a hill before us stands the cabin he built a hundred years ago. Call it the final home of a prodigal son. His father had 23 children and title to a treasure: six thousand acres of rolling Tennessee countryside, a grant for service in the Revolution. The girls in the family married into every other family on the plateau; their progeny filled cemeteries. But the grandfather was the only boy to reach adulthood. He got the land, all of it, and with all due haste, got rid of it. Sold it down to 37 acres in his lifetime.

But here's the harder part to understand. He left Tennessee in his youth and went to Missouri. No one knows why. When the war came, he was drafted into Lincoln's army, thereafter cursing Lincoln's name. For reasons again unclear, he returned to Tennessee, perhaps to reclaim his old life while starting anew. That's when he built the cabin just across the creek from where a grandson now lives.

The grandfather played the fiddle in his final years and ordered his whiskey by mail. He was something of a lawyer; he had read a bit and even argued a few cases. He was something of a dentist; anyone needing a tooth pulled, he pulled it. The motives for his wayward life he took to the grave. He left behind the cabin, the 37 acres, the fiddle, an old tintype photo, and the questions — all of it creating for the grandson a rich if strange legacy and sense of place.

How long have you been among us: five generations or five years? What story have you to tell?

Some of us arrived in frontier times, crossing the passes from Carolina and Virginia. Before that we were herders in Scotland and Ireland, and we were tough as you had to be when someone could rustle your wealth. We were fiercely independent, forming on Tennessee soil the first governing association free of British rule on the continent. We were acquisitive, rapidly staking the fertile bottomland, moving up the gentle slopes, claiming the broad plateau, and pressing ever west. We kept the stirring ballads of the Highlands and danced like kilted soldiers, feet a skipping blur and arms braced to our sides.

Some of us had been here for centuries. Our small towns lined the banks of rivers. We, too, had our laws and languages, our creation stories and temples. We were hunters and fishermen who traveled vast grounds in search of game, sometimes warring with one another. Later, we built log homes and planted gardens and schooled our children. The newcomers pressing west took more and more of our land by treaty. Finally, they drove us from our homes, penned us in stockades, and sent us forever from Tennessee. Only our melodic names given to rivers and cities and the state itself survived.

Some of us came as chattel. Plucked from our villages, we made the 80-day crossing in the fetid holds of ships. We were torn from our families, sold in the market, and sent to the fine pillared homes with their giant tobacco and cotton spreads. Some of us worked in the fields; others served in the house. As we labored, we sang of freedom as did the Children in Pharaoh's land.

Our grandson wrote of our journey. He heard the haunting tales of the African from his grandmother and great aunts as they talked into the summer evenings on the front porch in Henning. He combed through slaveship manifests in distant libraries and followed the story to Gambia, piecing it together. He made us all more aware of our roots, how important it is to know who came before and what they achieved.

The writer's boyhood friend is now the mayor of Henning. He grew up with the aspirations of his kinfolk whispered in his ears. "We knew our teachers could lead us from ignorance," he says. "When they were strict, we didn't complain. We thought the greatest privilege in the world was to go to school. My teacher said her mission was to rob the field of field hands. We'd talk about who we'd be like. We chose lofty people. The dreams were

so deep in a little Negro boy and girl."

We came as free men, black and white, to build bridges and railroads as commerce

thrived. We returned to our plundered homes as the remnant of a beaten army to start anew.

We came as carpetbaggers. Even through the smoke and desolation of war, we saw the richness

of the land, and the entrepreneurial spirit stirred within us. We replanted our families from the

North and started farms and orchards, banks and foundries.

We came in flight from famine and poverty and persecution. We came from Russia,

Germany and Ireland, Poland, Greece and Italy. We, too, were pioneers. Our cabins were

the teeming tenements of New York's Lower East Side. Following a trail often blazed by

family members and friends, we moved to Tennessee. We took jobs as cooks and painters,

farmhands and peddlers.

My grandparents were immigrants. They acquired mom-and-pop stores and bustled

about their businesses in a new tongue salted with Old-World expressions. They worked hard,

harder than others so as to gain a foothold in the land. They treasured its freedom, its promise,

its attitudes. They were judged on their merits. Where they came from was less important to

their neighbor than where they were going. And they never looked back.

The geography of our Tennessee home shaped us. We grew partial to a particular

landscape and climate, speech and custom. In the cities, we developed an outgoing

friendliness. In small towns, we learned everyone by name. In the country, we waved at all

who passed. Where houses were few, we kept watch on our neighbors. When disaster

struck, we banded together, clothing a burned-out family or helping a burdened farmer bring

in a crop. After all, they would do the same for us.

3 3

We are the old ones who left Tennessee and returned. We have seen and done it all.

Now we sit mornings in a general store to chew on the past. Once upon a time, our little

town thrived. There was work to be had in the big mill and the mines. When they closed,

we had to go north to find jobs at construction sites and auto plants. But we each came back.

Why? This is home, simple as that. But let us put it less sentimentally for you: "Even an old

dog, if you treat it half right, will wander back."

We welcome the newcomers from sister states and abroad, for they enrich us. Often

they see what we miss. They grow quiet as they crest our mountains, and they pause to read the

inscriptions on our battlefield monuments. They slow for the blazing green of our summer fields

and the iced green of our rushing creeks. They listen to our stories with a sharper ear. Historic

homes and shops that have been left to crumble, they rescue, nursing them back to elegant life.

To them, we are the prodigals, the spendthrifts of our beauty and history. They renew us by

reminding us what we have and who we are and what we ought to be.

Harlinsdale Farm, Franklin

Left: Bedford County

Pages 34 & 35: Franklin
Previous spread: Miss Mary Bobo's Boarding House, Lynchburg

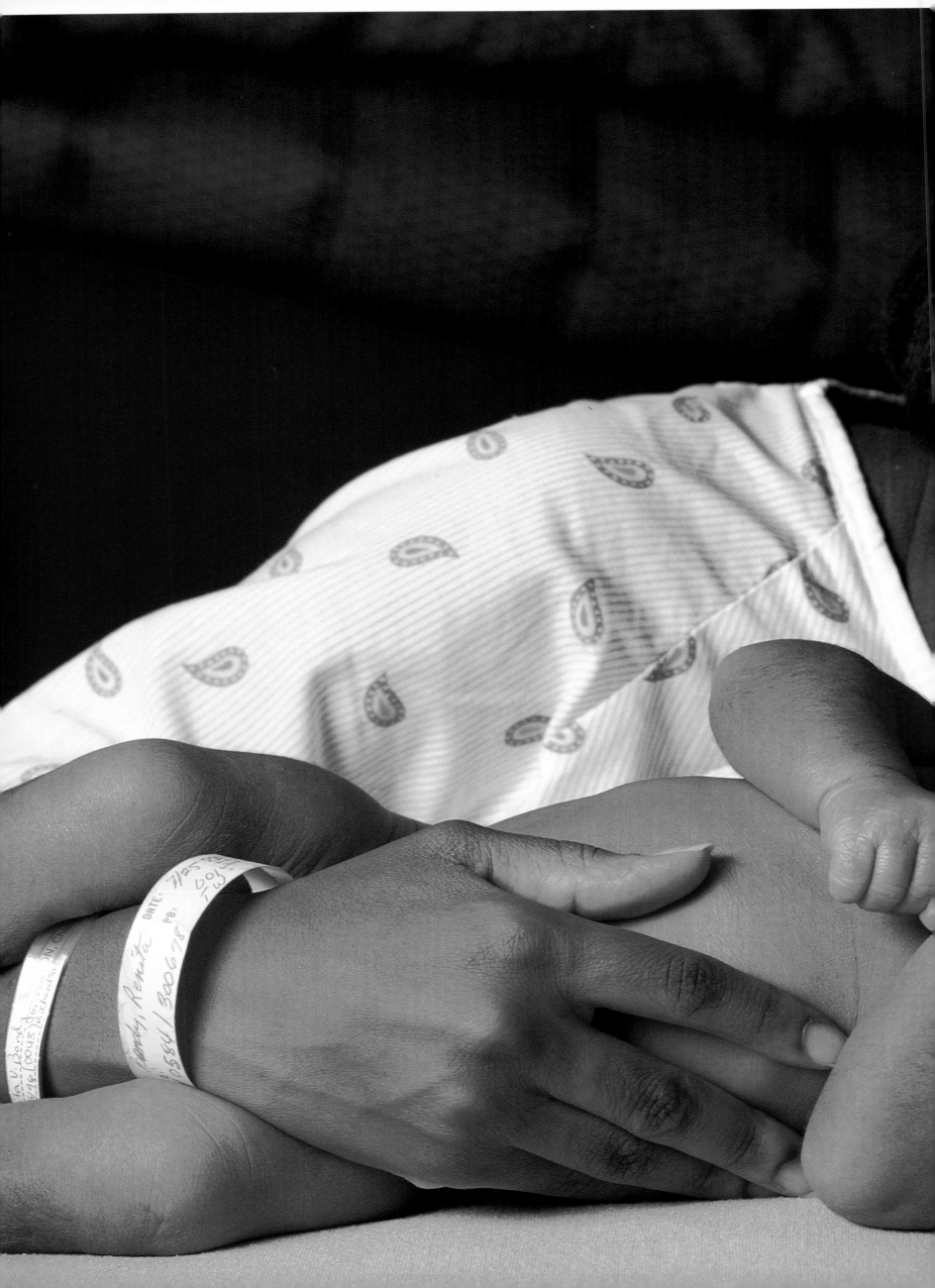

Columbia

Right: Museum of Appalachia, Norris

Williamson County

Left: Franklin

"IN THE CITIES, WE DEVELOPED AN OUTGOING FRIENDLINESS.
IN SMALL TOWNS, WE LEARNED EVERYONE BY NAME.
IN THE COUNTRY, WE WAVED AT ALL WHO PASSED."

Main Street, Franklin

Left: Franklin

writes a Sunday column of wit and wisdom, and everything is grist: marriage, family,

friendship, respect, courage, hope, and passion. "It's where the action is," he says of his perch

IN THE LAND OF WORK

We plunge into the land of work and find it in the apple-scented coolness

New Harmony, Walden Ridge

Right: Oren Wooden, Wooden's Apple Orchard, Walden Ridge

Previous spread: Harlinsdale Farm, Franklin

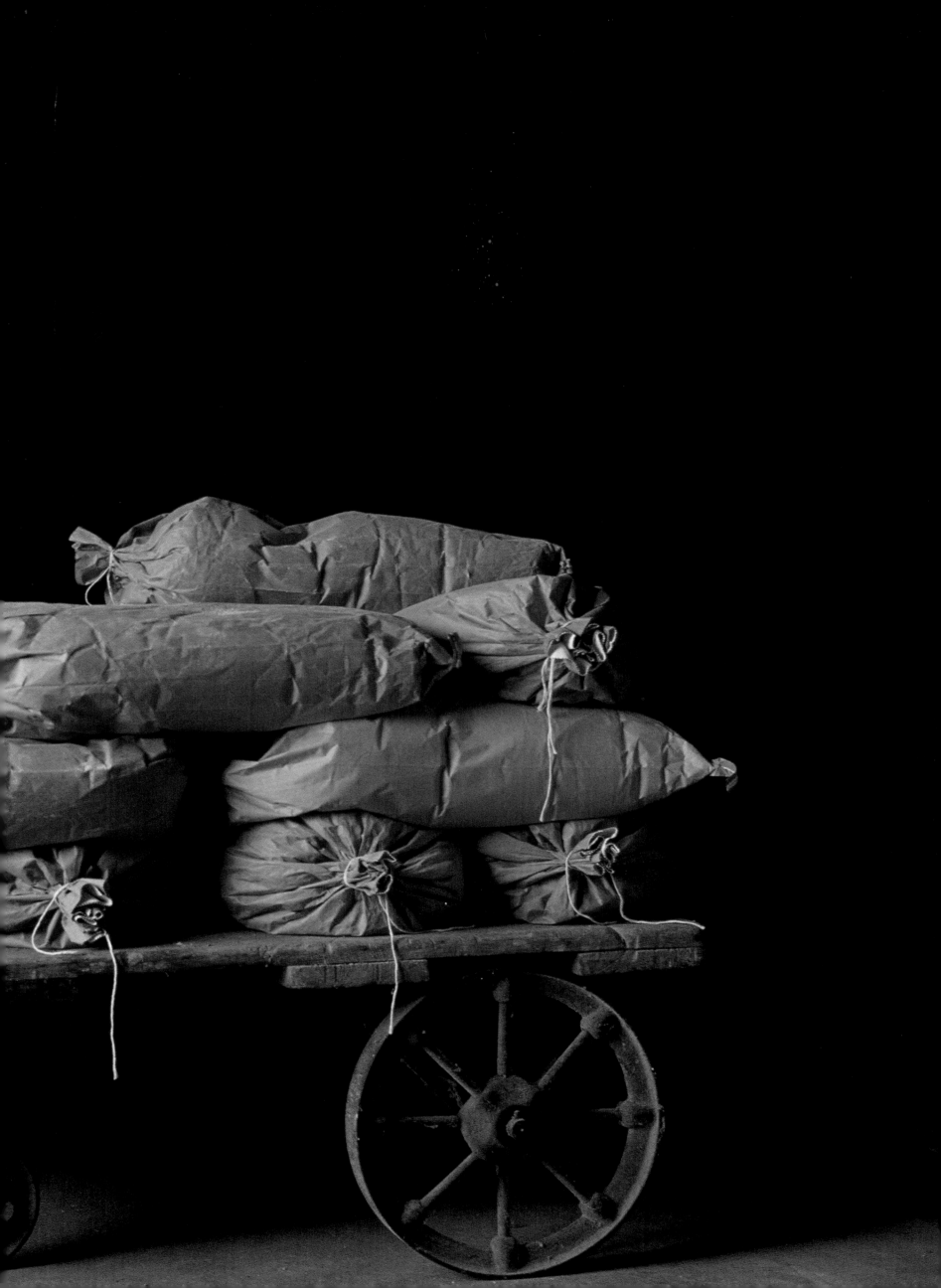

Carter's Creek Pike, Burwood

Previous spread: William Janey, miller at Falls Mill, est. 1873, near Winchester

"WE COME FOR THE OLD MEN FINGERING THEIR CARDS
AND THE QUICK-FINGERED WOMEN PLANTING FLOWERS
ON EMBROIDERED SPREADS."

Norris

63

Lynchburg town square

Left: Ken Huff and son, Charlie, Huff's Market, est. 1911, Burwood

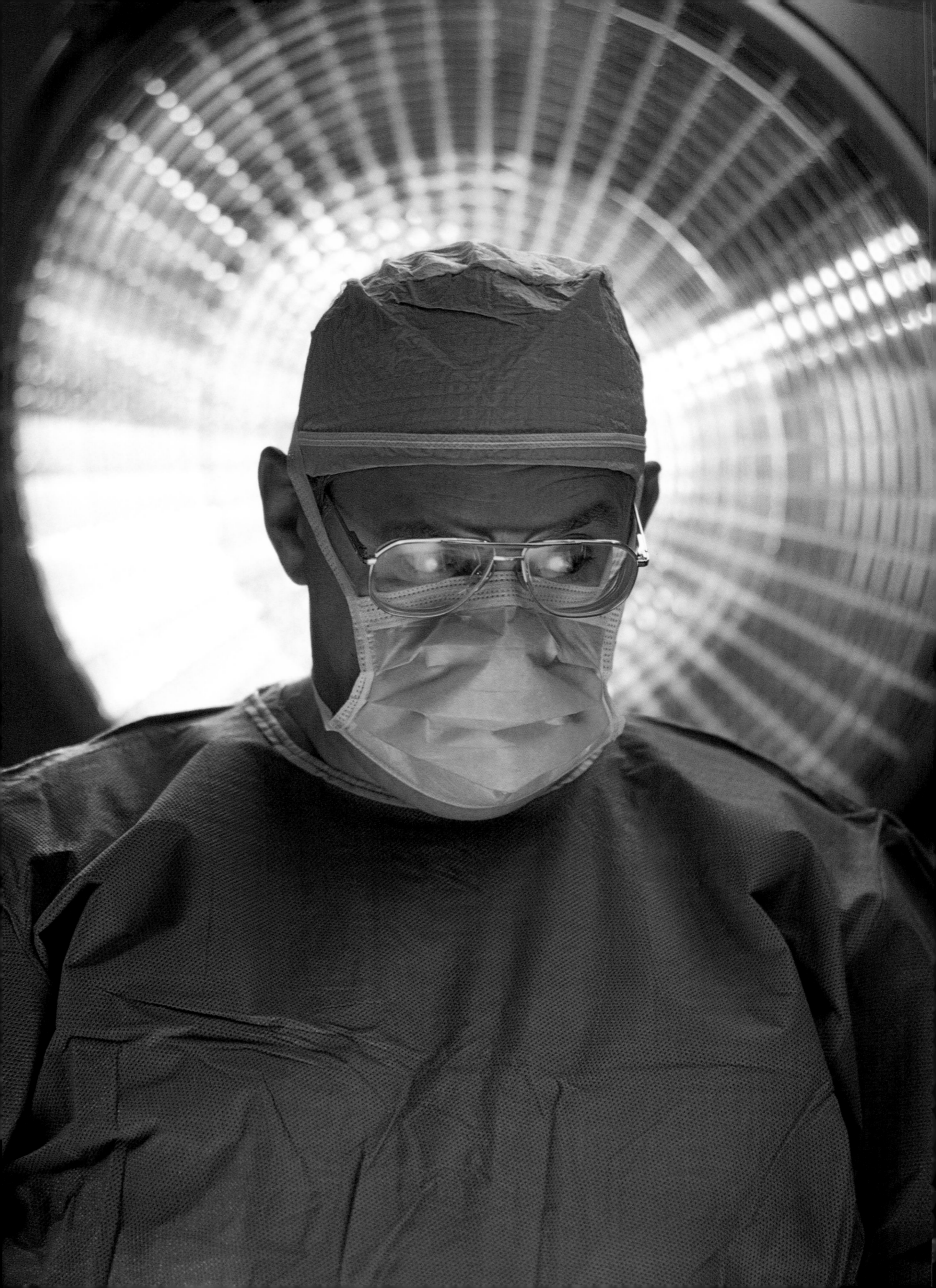

Cross Mountain, Campbell County

Left: Chattanooga

Cancer technology, Chattanooga

Left: Medical residents, Memphis

Previous spread: Bud Ellis, carousel carver, Chattanooga
Following spread: Jim Sherraden, Hatch Show Print, Nashville

Harlinsdale Farm, Franklin

Left: Leipers Fork, Williamson County
Following spread: Alan LeQuire, Nashville

THE SPIRIT OF PLAY

An old man in bib overalls leans patiently against a wall. Above him, a second-hand ticks its way across a large studio clockface, but he pays it no attention. In the dark and curtained corner where he stands, he exchanges small talk with the man next to him as casually as a worker waiting to punch in at the start of a shift. This is work for Brother Oswald, in the strict sense, but you must also believe this is play.

At his cue, he saunters from the wings into the blinding light of center stage and takes a seat facing a national TV audience. Host Porter Wagoner introduces the veteran Opry performer and speaks in admiration of the signature sound he coaxes from the dobro. Brother Oswald does not disappoint. He produces a delicate wash of notes that has the audience hushed and then cheering and Wagoner shaking his head in wonderment. For all the animation on Oswald's face, he might be tinkering with the belt on a tractor. But his reserve only heightens our appreciation for what he does.

At the heart of our play is love and admiration. We love the music we listen to and appreciate those who make it and make it well. We love sports. Football is followed with a fervency close to religion, but we can be zealots for other sports, too. We feast on our countryside: we love the dappled trails we walk and the dense woods we hunt and the glassy inlets we fish. We love people who play well at anything: tossing horseshoes or landing bass, riding a Walker or throwing a perfect Saturday afternoon spiral pass.

We love the animals that are part of our play. They gaze nobly at us from twenty-thousand-dollar portraits in the National Birddog Museum at Grand Junction. Here, we honor an animal bred to herd sheep in the days before the Pharaohs, and its lovers across America send mementos of their champions' careers to be enshrined in this place. Their names and winning dates are engraved on chalices and etched in glass. This is about love and blood lines. In breeding, we're told, goodness begets goodness, and sorry begets sorry.

An auctioneer is talking of blood lines in Bedford County. The black mare on the block — That's My Baby — has good lineage and, he says, she's "sellin' sound in every way." Her black eyes smoke as sweat-stained young men on foot run her back and forth on the sawdust track in front of the covered stands. We listen to the auctioneer bid up the crowd: "Great mare; she's smart. She's got a good daddy and a good momma. She's as good a colt as there is in Shelbyville. Twenty-five...twenty-five, give me twenty-six. Everything on this mare is perfect: pedigree, confirmation; I defy anyone to tell me what to change." He raises the bar for a final offer. "Thirty-five'll knock his (top bidder's) head plum in the creek." But no taker at that price. He points to the stands, bringing down the gavel. "Sold her, thirty-thousand."

A horse's head arches upward in a silent whinny. On a shelf next to it, a hoofed leg kicks out to us, a torso lies on its side, and a tail flows like a torch flame. These parts are not of flesh but soft basswood, carved with love in an old building in Chattanooga, and waiting to be assembled. We're making horses at the only fulltime carousel carving school in America, and there's nothing but the limits of imagination to rein us in. To our carousel we add a frog in a suit, a high-stepping ostrich in top hat, a pig, a tiger, a giraffe.

People come here from everywhere: a man from Oregon, a couple from Boston, sisters from London, and from all walks of life: a trucker, a farmer, a secretary, an emergency room nurse — to bring life to these whimsical creations. Most of the artists have never held a carver's chisel in their lives. They're told only to bring a picture of their dream and not to worry; nothing can go wrong.   Should you lop an ear off, add putty and try again. It's the joy of releasing life from blocks of wood that enthralls them, and if your animal takes two years to finish, that's OK. The arched head, with bunched muscles in the neck and black orbs for eyes, will be here, waiting for its carver to return.

We love our pageantry, and no spectacle rivals game day. The band marches along Stadium Drive on a cold, sun-splashed November afternoon, the musicians wearing white plumes and spats, the majorettes covered in goosebumps and orange spangles. Black flutes and silver tubas wave from side to side to the drummer's beat, then are drawn to pursing lips to blare the bars of the fight song. The bright fall air is filled with the savory smell of hot dogs and relish and the milling excitement of the crowd. It's football time in Tennessee.

Earlier, the team made its ritual entry to the stadium. Dressed in slacks and blazers, the players walked down the hill from the main campus with few words between them. The coach, dressed in a business suit, was in the lead. He had weathered a week of criticism following a shocking loss, and there seemed a poignancy to his earnest expression. He looked straight ahead, both edgy and intent, like an attorney ready to argue his case. A jury of 104,000 waits in the stands, and they are joined by a million listeners across the state. We watch the game from the shady side of the fans and feel the girdered stadium shake to their stomping feet. It can barely contain the emotion, and this, not the cold, raises goosebumps now.

Our music was born in emotion. Blues is the voice of the soul, a naked lament. Suspecting his wife of cheating, a bluesman ponders the implication of his dog's strange behavior, never barking when a certain friend comes around. The singer may bark or slur the lyrics himself; it doesn't matter, if he and the guitar speak with emotion. Love songs and drinking songs and working-class anthems are in the country tradition. Listen to the Nashville sound: the words are crystal clear because the story is important, and the excitement comes from hearing a catchy ballad for the first time.

There are so many sounds rooted in our experience and recorded in our studios and so many ways to celebrate them. Some years ago in Memphis, two blocks and the space of a world separated Beale Street from the Peabody Hotel. With a few heard-earned dollars in their pockets, sharecroppers from the Delta came to party at Beale Street clubs, where the entertainment was as raucous as themselves. Plantation owners and well-heeled merchants checked into the Peabody, sipping drinks beside the marble fountain in the richly paneled lobby. Magically, the Peabody preserves the genteel atmosphere of the planter society. A stroll through and you feel anointed.

But give me the simple, the homegrown pleasures, you say. Then I give you walks in canyons of porcelain coolness and lazy floats down slow-moving rivers. I give you food, mountains of it. Here's what we bring to the old-time homecoming on the grounds of the church in the cove:

A huge meat loaf and crispy chicken that was dipped in flour and buttermilk and dipped again before it was fried. Vegetables fresh-picked from the garden: tons of tomatoes and cucumbers and squash; green beans flavored with ham, and corn kernels fried in bacon grease, and sweet potatoes baked with marshmallows arranged in a pattern. There's iced tea liberally sweetened and poured from gallon glass jars. For dessert, five kinds of cakes, four kinds of pies, three kinds of cobblers, egg custard and tubs of banana pudding.

Of the cakes, the coconut has to be tasted, for between each of its five yellow layers and all over the sides and top is a frosting of stiffened and sugared egg whites sprinkled with coconut, purchased in a distant town and freshly grated by hand. Some ancient woman of the cove, following a recipe of long ago, rose at 4 a.m. to make it for us, and it tastes of love.

Nashville

Pages 82 & 83: *Eighth Avenue, Nashville*
Previous spread: Oak Hill, Nashville

General Jackson, Cumberland River

Following spread: Pat McGee, advertising executive, Nashville

Grand Ole Opry, Nashville

Right: Tootsie's Orchid Lounge, Nashville

"COUNTRY SINGS OF LIFE'S BITTERSWEETNESS,
OF HUMOR AND HEARTACHE, IN PLAIN WORDS
AND CLEVER LYRICS."

Trey Bruce, songwriter, Green's Grocery, Leipers Fork

Right: Backstage, Clarence Brown Theatre, University of Tennessee, Knoxville

George Hunt, public school art teacher and painter of the blues, Memphis

Left: Blues singer Blind Mississippi Morris, at historic Ernastine and Hazel's hotel, Memphis

Hillsboro Hounds, Cornersville

Left: Iroquois Steeplechase, Nashville

Shoal Branch, Williamson County

Bean Hollow, Moore County

Williamson County

Previous spread: Volunteers versus Alabama, Neyland Stadium, Knoxville

Pacer mascot, University of Tennessee at Martin

Following spread: Fayetteville
Pages 106 & 107: Lynchburg

VISIT TO SACRED PLACES

Let us be witness, you and me, to tales of triumph and sorrow, to scenes

of beauty and faith. Let us begin with a 14-year-old, who leaves home to seek work beyond

the hills of Tennessee. Short of stature, large in heart, he wants not to burden his farming

parents, who must raise eight children on rocky soil. Like a biblical Jacob, he toils 14 years in

exile, shucking corn and raising cattle for others. Nearly every cent of his meager wage is

gathered for a dream. In time, he returns to Tennessee to buy the family farm.

Back home, always working, he prospers among the rocks and roots of the hillsides and

slowly adds to his holdings. When a town is sold at public auction, he buys more parcels of land.

But there are other investments to make. He and his wife, a teacher, assume guardianship of a

neighbor's 15 orphaned children, paying for a needed operation, placing them in homes, giving

them equal portions of their cared-for family farm when they come of age. Never does this little

man cease his labors, nor claim a rightful seat on the loafer's bench at the general store. Even in

wiry old age, driving cattle in his straw hat in the heat of summertime, he would outwork you.

How many of our people, like James Polk Irwin, the hero of the tale, have lifted

themselves and others from hardscrabble lives by dint of perseverance? Strong, humble,

resolute people run like a vein through the bedrock of the land. Passed to their children were

the gifts of humor and honesty, sacrifice and tenacity, gentleness and faith. Near the town of

Norris in Anderson County, where Polk Irwin lived, we visit the Museum of Appalachia and

find a shrine to their deeds.

What of the courage and resolve of those we visit in the vacant room of the

Victorian Gothic building on the university campus? Before us are seven young women and

four young men, most of them emancipated slaves. Their noble countenances are larger than

life in the room's wall-size portrait, commissioned by a British queen. In 1871, the Jubilee

Singers of Nashville's Fisk University began touring New England and Europe in concerts. Their mission was to raise money to save their beleaguered school, housed at the time in cramped wooden barracks that were salvaged from the war.

They feared ridicule for singing such plaintive Negro spirituals as "Go Down, Moses," "Turn Back Pharaoh's Army," and "Swing Low, Sweet Chariot." But the songs moved their audiences to tears and spread their fame across two continents. Like Joshua, they fought the battle, but their haunting melodies brought the brick walls and gabled roof and ornate bell tower of their new home, Jubilee Hall, tumbling up.

We move outdoors for another kind of music. It comes from the reverberation of rapids in a river gorge 500 feet below us, and it, too, is haunting. The Big South Fork of the Cumberland River carved this channel through the Cumberland Plateau and has played this music for thousands of years. We stand alone at the overlook and receive from the walls of the canyon the river's amplified tidings. This is one of our last wild places, and it is sacred to us.

We come to where the waters parted. In the winter of 1812, a series of immense earthquakes shook the northwest corner of the state. The earth rolled like ocean waves; Judgment Day tremblings rattled furniture in Knoxville and rang steeple bells still further away. As the Mississippi raged, the land near it sank, creating a shallow depression, and water belonging to the river split off and flowed into the basin. Reelfoot Lake inspires us with its powerful genesis and its strangeness, where cypress knees breathe above the shallow waters of a wild floating garden.

But nature can shake us more powerfully still. A baby is dying; no one's fault. The heart is defective and can't be repaired. His whole life will pass in the arc of a day. He seems to know, for his eyes have grown old. But the young mother and father want to remember his stay. The family — grandmother, cousins, uncles, aunts — gather with parents and child for a picture.

There is strange disjointed laughter in the hospital room, and eyes filled with tears. The father laughs when the baby jerks in startled response to the camera's flash. That night the baby dies in the nursery, and the world grows dark. The father quietly rocks his lifeless son for two hours to some inward melody, and the nurses let them be. This place, too, is sacred in its grief.

We come to read our cemeteries. The old ones tell their stories in split and weathered stone. We see faintly etched the dates of the young woman who died in childbirth, and the child who followed three weeks after. There is the year of the epidemic, when rich and poor were laid to rest; the plague can be read like the ring on a tree. There are cemeteries to the four years of slaughter; row upon row of nameless blocks above the graves of nameless men. The anonymous fallen of both sides now march into memory together. In another cemetery is the trampled but still standing fence that separates one race from another, as if to say, even in death do us part.

We part, too, at the church's curved staircase. It leads to the balcony where the house servants stayed while their owners sat below in wooden pews. What message did the pastor bring these antebellum Sundays in LaGrange? Who drew comfort and who grew restless in the gaze of the gold-leaf inscription above the pulpit: THOU GOD SEEST ME?

We visit the scene of a battle, for all such places are sacred ground. We are north of Memphis on the wooded Chickasaw Bluffs above the Mississippi. Six hundred Union troops were stationed here, at Fort Pillow, controlling river passage from the promontory. Some were Tennessee Unionists, scorned by fellow Tennesseans as "home grown Yankees;" half were black troops, considered property to be returned.

The war was but a year from over in April 1864 when Confederate General Nathan Bedford Forrest rode after the garrison's horses and supplies. His 1,500 men stole up the steep ravine below the fort, and a sharpshooter killed the Union commander as he peered above the breastworks. Believing reinforcements were imminent, the second in command refused to

surrender. Enraged by his answer and the alleged taunts of the defenders, Forrest's men stormed

the fort. They set with fury upon the panicked troops in their headlong retreat down the face of

the bluff to the river. Tennessean fell upon Tennessean. On this day there would be no refuge

from the rage of the Soldiers of the Lost Cause.

We come, though, not to argue the cause or what the fighting was most about. We

come to say insanity and gallantry often shared the battlefield. It is the selfless acts that we recall

and chisel into the pediments of the granite spires that dot our landscape. The declaration on

the courthouse monument in Paris would apply equally to the soldiers of both sides: "No

country ever had truer sons; no cause nobler champions."

We hear shouting, but no longer is it war. A man in the audience is speaking in

tongues. The tabernacle of believers is hushed as the preacher on the platform translates the

utterance. The Pentecostal spirit is with us tonight, we're told, and music and joy break out.

The crowd is flowing forward to be touched by the spirit and cleansed of sickness and sin. The

preacher's hands are on fire; believers shake in mad spasms and fall limp to the floor. Slowly, the

tremors pass. May we still shake with purpose and good works when we go home.

Still in the land of faith, we sing a melody simple as a lullaby. "Bim, bom; Bim bim bim

bom; Bim bim bim bim bim bom." It is brotherhood and sisterhood week, and we are in

synagogue seats, cloaked in the ecumenical spirit. We are black and white, Protestant, Catholic,

Baha'i and Jew, Tennesseans all, and we are clapping in time and singing in unison to the melody

with the simple refrain: "Shabbat shalom."

Ephemeral as a flame, the vision of Sabbath peace dances before us.

"IT IS THE SELFLESS ACTS OF WAR THAT WE RECALL
AND CHISEL INTO THE PEDIMENTS OF THE GRANITE SPIRES
THAT DOT OUR LANDSCAPE."

Confederate Cemetery, Carnton Mansion, Franklin

Right: Confederate monument, town square, Franklin

Previous spread: Mount Mingus, Great Smoky Mountains

Rachel Jackson's Garden, The Hermitage

Left: The Hermitage, home of Andrew Jackson, Nashville

Previous spread: Carter House plantation office, most battle-scarred building on American soil, Franklin

All Saints' Chapel, University of the South, Sewanee

Right: Armory Room, Masonic Hall, circa 1823, Franklin: site of Andrew Jackson's treaty signing with the Chickasaw Nation

Previous spread: Fisk University Jubilee Singers, Nashville

State Capitol, Nashville

Right: Vietnam Veteran's Memorial, War Memorial Plaza, State Capitol, Nashville

...DONALD K SGT USA
MATTHEWS THOMAS W JR 1LT USA
MATTHEWS WILLIS A PFC USA
MATTOCK JOHN L CPL USA
MAYS JAMES JR SP4 USA
McARTHUR ROBERT L PFC USA
McBROOM EDDIE O JR PFC USA
McCALL CLAIBORNE P 1STLT USAF
McCARRELL JOHN E SGT USA
McCARTER JERRY PFC USMC
McCARTER ROBERT L PFC USA
McCARTER THOMAS L HN USN
McCORKLE BENNIE E SP4 USA
McCORMICK DONNIE R SP4 USA
McCORMICK RONNIE L PFC USMC
McCULLOUGH BEN JR PFC USA

McKINNEY
McLEMO
McLOUGH
McMURTT
McNEAL
McNISH J
McPHAIL
McREE JO
McREYNO
MEADE JO
MEDLEY
MEEK DO
MEISTER
MELTON
MEREDITH
MERONE
MERREL

ON THE RIM OF THE WORLD

They are ghostly in the vaporish air — a doe and a fawn standing

still as statuary 6,000 feet up the Smokies on the Appalachian Trail. Muffled in my poncho,

absorbed in my thoughts, I've stumbled on their path. Now I hold perfectly still, alert and

quiet in their gaze. A long moment passes; no one moves. Finally, unhurried, doe and fawn

turn away with courtly gait and vanish in the velvet mist.

Are they real or spirit form? In these mountains, it is fair to ask. The fastness of the

densely wooded coves and the mist rising like fires from the flanks inspire reverence, and

mystery. To the Cherokees, this land was home to the Little People, spiritual guides who

imparted wisdom to those who approached with a purified heart. Remove your easy assumptions,

cast off your corporeal thoughts; you tread on mystical ground.

So remote are these mountains that hikers have strayed but a few yards from the trail

to become lost in the endlessly repeating folds — each like a room fancily furnished to the

whims of its micro climate, mostly poplars in this ravine, birches in that — never to be seen

again. So strange is this land that the trees standing as sentinels on high ridges are Canadian

exiles, their seed pushed a thousand miles south by glacial sheets far to the north, and

marooned on these islands of coolness as the ice retreated. So lofty are the mountaintops they

have never felt the drilling heat of a Southern summer.

We are at the headwaters of life. Gray galleons of clouds run aground on these peaks,

loosing their cargo, the evaporated freight of the ocean, in drumming sheets. Leaves and

branches and blades of grass bead heavy with drops that find the earth and fuse like quicksilver

and race to swollen streams. Fanning over ledges, they drop from the mountains with a muffled

roar and grow to rivers that spread in the valleys below and flow once more to the sea.

From the salamander to the bear, life here is fecund. And there is no guile. You may be crushed by a hemlock or bitten by a rattler or swept away by a raging stream, but that is nature's blind force at work. Nothing here means you ill. Only arrogance or ignorance or bad luck will undo you.

The pioneers came to these mountains with hope and grit. You can still see indentations on the earth where their wagons, jouncing with cares and expectations, crossed a lofty gap. The timber companies came with calculating greed, measuring the virgin forests in board feet and leaving behind ruination. The settlers came with pluck. They farmed in Cades Cove and drove their animals to summer pasture in the luxuriant grass on Spence's Field half a mile above. The herders carved their initials and dates in stones that stand witness to those dreamy quiet days on the lip of the world.

Many years ago, I came to the mountains as a pilgrim in search of something I knew not existed. I slung a bulging Army surplus knapsack to my shoulders and trudged off from Davenport Gap, six days of hiking before me. Crossing a farmer's field, I gained the mountain path and began the long climb. Up, up I went, swaying like a pack animal under the heavy load.

My heart beat like a tom-tom, my shoulders sagged from the pack's weight, my thighs burned from the strain of the climb. Why was I here? What good reason for all this work? I marched on. As I rounded still another switchback, the earth suddenly opened. Before me were the Smokies, wave after wave of crenelated mountains with long sloping ridges and crimped peaks, dark green in the foreground and growing soft blue in the miles of hazy distance.

Living cloistered in Tennessee's green valleys, nothing prepared me for such immense open space. I stood hushed, listening to the sounds of a stream in the distance and the wind in the crowns of a million trees. A hawk rode a thermal; the air shimmered. The sweep and depth of the vista beckoned. I imagined myself able to step from the trail into the ocean of space and float with the hawk high above the canting ridges and ravines. Fatigue vanished. The spirit

soared. A door opened and life was enlarged.

The Smokies are kindling for the soul, and — even queued in traffic on two-lane

Highway 441 that lies like a ribbon across the mountains — you feel the spark. Press your hand to

the windshield. The air grows cooler as you gain elevation. At 3,000 feet you pass cove hardwood

forests with virgin stands of maple, poplar and hemlock. A cascading stream lines the road. Roll

down the window and feel the wash of mountain air with its rich scent of needles and duff.

Leave your car and head up a trail and into a cove. Go far enough to be long out of

earshot of traffic and your neighbor and look about. Find moss-covered rocks as padded as

ottomans and jumbled roots as hard and polished as teak. Stand where the towering

hardwoods split the morning light. Watch water cascade over polished rock in a glittering

necklace of light. Come face to face with a doe and her fawn on a high ridge in the morning

mist. Love the moment. And stand very, very still.

Right: Roaring Fork, Great Smoky Mountains

Following spread: Newfound Gap, Great Smoky Mountains

Anderson County

Left: New Harmony, Walden Ridge

Previous spread: Museum of Appalachia, Norris

Knoxville

Previous spread: Troy Webb, retired coal miner and folk art carver, Claiborne County

Cades Cove Methodist Church, Great Smoky Mountains

John Oliver Cabin, Cades Cove, Great Smoky Mountains

Previous spread: Cane Creek Cascades, Fall Creek Falls State Park

Gene Horner, master fiddle maker, Cumberland Plateau

"WE STAND IN THE GOLDEN DUST OF LATE AFTERNOON LIGHT...
IT IS A TIME WHEN WE UNDERSTAND THIS LAND
IS TOO FINE FOR YOU AND ME. THAT WE DON T OWN IT.
RATHER, IT POSSESSES US."

West Prong of Little Pigeon River, Sugarland Mountain, Great Smoky Mountains